Achieving True Success

How to Build Character as a Family

A Fence or an Ambulance

'Twas a dangerous cliff, as they freely confessed,
Though to walk near its crest was so pleasant;
But over its terrible edge there had slipped
A duke and full many a peasant.
So the people said something would have to be done,
But their projects did not at all tally;
Some said, "Put a fence around the edge of the cliff,"
Some, "An ambulance down in the valley."

But the cry for the ambulance carried the day,
For it spread through the neighboring city;
A fence may be useful or not, it is true,
But each heart became brimful of pity
For those who slipped over that dangerous cliff;
And the dwellers in highway and alley
Gave pounds or gave pence, not to put up a fence,
But an ambulance down in the valley.

"For the cliff is all right, if you're careful," they said,
"And, if folks even slip and are dropping,
It isn't the slipping that hurts them so much,
As the shock down below when they're stopping."
So day after day, as these mishaps occurred,
Quick forth would those rescuers sally
To pick up the victims who fell off the cliff,
With their ambulance down in the valley.

Then an old sage remarked: "It's a marvel to me
That people give far more attention
To repairing results than to stopping the cause,
When they'd much better aim at prevention.
Let us stop at its source all this mischief," cried he,
"Come, neighbors and friends, let us rally;
If the cliff we will fence we might almost dispense
With the ambulance down in the valley." . . .

Better guide well the young than reclaim them when old,
For the voice of true wisdom is calling,
"To rescue the fallen is good, but 'tis best
To prevent other people from falling."
Better close up the source of temptation and crime
Than deliver from dungeon or galley;
Better put a strong fence round the top of the cliff
Than an ambulance down in the valley.

Joseph Malins

Achieving True Success

How to Build Character as a Family

This book belongs to . . .

THE

_____

FAMILY

Published by International Association of Character Cities (IACC), a division of Character Training Institute, Inc.
520 West Main Street • Oklahoma City, OK 73102-2220 • Tel: 405-815-0001 • Fax: 405-815-0002 • info@characterfamilies.org • www.characterfirst.com

Achieving True Success: How to Build Character as a Family
Published by International Association of Character Cities
A division of Character Training Institute, Inc.

For information:
International Association of Character Cities
A division of Character Training Institute, Inc.
520 West Main Street
Oklahoma City, OK 73102-2220
Tel: 405-815-0001
Fax: 405-815-0002
info@charactercities.org
www.charactercities.org

Library of Congress Control Number: 00-101679

International Standard Book Number: 0-9679941-0-1 (hardbound)

Printed in the United States of America
Second Edition
06 07 08 09 10 11 — 10 9 8 7 6 5 4 3 2 1

Achieving True Success

Contents

character in nature and the home
17

building character as a community
70

kids excited about character
72

How to Build Character as a Family

character

n. [Gr. charakter, "to scrape, cut, engrave"]

By way of eminence, distinguished or good qualities; those which are esteemed and respected; and those which are ascribed to a person in common estimation

Webster's 1828 Dictionary

"A good character is more valuable than gold."

Anonymous

What is character?

Determination
Purposing to accomplish right goals at the right time, regardless of the opposition

Character is the inward motivation to do what is right, whatever the cost. Every person on earth has equal opportunity to build his or her character by working on qualities such as truthfulness, patience, and loyalty. When daily decisions are based on these qualities, you will experience practical and lasting rewards.

"A man's character is his fate."
Heraclitus

"The measure of a man's real character is what he would do if he knew he would never be found out."
Baron Thomas Babington Macaulay

"I am what I am today because of the choices I made yesterday."
Anonymous

"The final forming of a person's character lies in their own hands."
Anne Frank

If there is righteousness in the heart,
   there will be beauty in character,
If there is beauty in character,
   there will be harmony in the home.
If there is harmony in the home,
   there will be order in the nation;
If there is order in the nation,
   there will be peace in the world.

Chinese proverb

Diligence
Investing my time and energy to complete each task assigned to me

"Sow a thought,
  you reap an act;
sow an act,
  you reap a habit;
sow a habit,
  you reap a character;
sow a character,
  you reap a destiny."
Samuel Smiles

What is a Character Family?

Character Family is a family with challenges and pressures; with imperfections, inconsistencies, and needs; with periodic conflicts and failures
***but** a family that has purposed to learn true harmony and genuine appreciation for each other and those outside the family.*

"The foundations of national morality must be laid in private families."—John Adams

HAVE YOU EVER WONDERED WHY some families seem to get along with each other and find true contentment and happiness, while others are ravaged by anger, bitterness, and division? The difference is not money, education, or opportunities. The difference is character. Some families, for example, are very poor, yet are truly successful in terms of family relationships. There are also wealthy families who have never experienced true peace and happiness.

In spite of unprecedented technological developments, there is a growing concern that we are failing in the most important of all achievements—building stronger families.

Points to ponder . . .

WE HAVE TALLER BUILDINGS but shorter tempers.

WE HAVE MORE CONVENIENCES but less time.

WE HAVE MORE KNOWLEDGE but less judgment.

WE HAVE FANCIER HOUSES but broken homes.

WE CLEAN UP OUR AIR but pollute our souls.

WE TRAVEL TO THE MOON but not to our neighbors.

WE ADD YEARS TO LIFE but not life to years.

—Source unknown

This book is designed to encourage you toward the wise and rewarding goal of building character. Read on to learn how you can begin . . .

Building a Character Family
. . . one choice at a time.

"I have a dream that my four children will one day live in a nation where they will not be judged by the color of their skin but by the content of their character."
Martin Luther King, Jr.

Does your family QUALIFY?

- Do you have occasional tensions or problems in your family?

- Are there things about other members of your family that irritate you?

- Do you tend to collect clutter around your home?

- Do you sometimes wish you could be in a different family?

- Do you find it hard to maintain a schedule in your daily activities?

- Is it difficult to get the whole family together for even a simple meal?

If you answer "YES" to one or more of these questions and believe that character is important for your family, then you qualify to become a Character Family!

Calling All Families
This Program Is for You!

Character is important for people of any age all around the world. Qualities such as creativity, patience, and generosity benefit the lives of both children and adults. Therefore, *every* family—regardless of size, social status, race, religion, or situation—can benefit from focusing on building character together. The Character Family idea is simply a tool that families can use to center their lives around qualities that bring success. It is designed, not to be a burden or "something else" to add to a busy schedule, but as a way to view life from a positive perspective and strengthen the family.

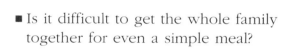

any family can build character

"To educate a person in mind and not in morals is to educate a menace to society."
Teddy Roosevelt

How can you build a Character Family?

"Travel east or west, a man's own house is still the best."—Robert Schumann

Character building as a family can be boiled down to four essential steps:

- Evaluate your **PERSPECTIVE** toward your family.
- Formulate a **PLAN** for developing character together.
- Begin to **PRACTICE** the basic principles of character building.
- Develop a **PROCEDURE** with practical steps of action.

Building a Character Family *step by step*

PHASE I: PERSPECTIVE

1 *Take responsibility* for your family.

Every parent has a choice between mediocrity and excellence in the home. Decide whether you will face your responsibilities and make your family your first priority or run from your responsibilities and watch yourself and your family pay the consequences.

2 *Decide* to aim for a successful home.

Success in the home is achieved by examining the way things are right now, setting your sights on the way they should be, and making the investments necessary to get from where you are to where you want to be. Short-term "loss" of time, energy, and convenience—if properly directed—will result in long-term gain for the whole family.

3 *Make the connection* between character and success.

The most powerful motivation for developing character is the connection between a person's goals and the character qualities necessary to achieve these goals. For example, if becoming a truck driver is the goal, a few qualities to focus on would be *attentiveness* in watching the road and traffic, *responsibility* in safely transporting others' goods, and *punctuality* in reaching the destination on time. It is essential to realize that your family will not achieve true success without character.

4 *Make a personal commitment* to character development.

Until a leader is committed, the followers probably won't be. Commit yourself to develop your own character first and foremost. Not only is this approach the basis of leadership, but your children will be watching you even more closely after you become a Character Family. They will learn more from your example than from anything else. Don't let this fact scare you away from becoming a Character Family. On the contrary, let it motivate you.

> "I am only one, but still I am one. I cannot do everything, but I can do something; and because I cannot do everything I will not refuse to do the something that I can do."
>
> Edward Everett Hale

1 *Step back* and take a careful look at your home life. Evaluate it. What strengths do you see? What weaknesses? Make a list of each. Then list the character qualities that target each weakness and enhance each strength.

- In identifying weaknesses, ask yourself these questions: If I had the power to change anything about myself or my family, what would it be? What are the things that irritate me about myself or my family? After identifying these needs, relate them back to character deficiencies. For example, if the house is continually a mess, this would show a need for orderliness, diligence, thoroughness, and responsibility.

2 *Make a list of goals* for your family, with a set of objectives for reaching each goal. If you aim for nothing, you will surely hit it.

- Picture the ideal family. This may require more effort for those who did not grow up in one. It is wise to get counsel from the members of other families you look up to as being successful. Then write out goals for your own family.

3 *Sketch a plan* for the pace, order, and method your Character Family will follow. Focusing on one quality per month works best for most people. Having a plan before beginning is critical in reaching the goals you have set and in giving you the confidence you need as a leader.

- Periodically evaluate your Character Family program to check your progress on meeting your goals and keeping on track.

Ideas & Projects
for Character Families

Return lost coins to the store clerk when shopping.

- Have children draw pictures and create posters for the home that depict different character qualities.

- Show gratefulness by making your own thank-you cards for those who have benefited your family.

- Take food and good cheer to the elderly and shut-ins in your area.

- Institute character recognition to acknowledge those who exhibit specific character qualities. Set aside times when each family member can praise another for a quality he or she saw demonstrated during the week.

- Use verbal reminders in everyday situations; for example, "What character quality will enable you to take out the trash with a good attitude?"

- Integrate discussions about character into family meals, story time, etc.

- Exercise creativity and come up with your own good ideas of how to weave character training into everyday life. Send them to us, so we can share them with other Character Families around the nation and throughout the world!

Label children's storybooks with the quality taught through the message of the book. For example, The Three Little Pigs—diligence.

> "**Character cannot be developed in ease and quiet. Only through experience of trial and suffering can the soul be strengthened, ambition inspired, and success achieved.**"
>
> Helen Keller

Building a Character Family *step by step*

Successful character training includes the following elements:

1 Modeling good character

Character is taught best as the parents model good character. Character growth is encouraged in children through recognizing, requiring, and emphasizing right attitudes, words, and actions. As parents model good character, children can see a living example of how to demonstrate good behavior.

- Of course, you as a parent are not going to be perfect. Ask forgiveness when you fail to demonstrate specific qualities and then be accountable to family members. Developing your own character is the first step in developing the character of those around you. The best way to teach is by example: it works a lot better to pull a string than to push it.

2 Praising good character

Everyone has a need for approval. Praising character both meets this need and provides motivation to continue demonstrating good character. Praise is pointing to words, actions, and attitudes that exemplify character qualities and explaining how they have benefited you or others. The goal is to help family members reach their full potential by praising good character.

- Since character determines our actions, it is more beneficial to praise character rather than achievement. Siblings may feel tension and competition among one another when parents praise achievement over character. If Johnny was praised for the achievement of getting good grades, Susie may feel envious or discouraged because she doesn't make good grades. But if Johnny was praised

for his *diligence* at school, Susie will then be motivated to do her own schoolwork diligently as well. Everyone has equal capacity to exercise good character.

> PRAISING ACHIEVEMENT VS.
> ## Praising Character
> - Achievement: "Your room looks good—thanks for cleaning it."
>   Character: "Thank you for your orderliness and enthusiasm in cleaning your room. I can tell you put your whole heart into it."
>   ("Getting the job done" may allow for cutting corners, like stuffing junk under beds and in closets, while character will not.)
> - Achievement: "You were so great to win your soccer game. You showed them!"
>   Character: "You showed such endurance and perseverance in your soccer game. Thank you for sticking in there even when it got tough."
>
> *for example*

3 Teaching good character

One of the most effective ways to teach character is to define and explain a character quality by connecting it to something that is memorable and makes a lasting impression. For example, if a child demonstrates laziness, a parent can teach him or her about the characteristics of the beaver. Showing the child how the beaver exercises *diligence* and what things the beaver does to be diligent will lead him

> "Actions cannot be called good unless they proceed from good motives."
> Noah Webster

or her to understand the nature of this quality. It would be important to relate these things to a real life situation for the child. Later, when he or she is being lazy or has been assigned a task, you need only say, "Remember the beaver," or, "Let's see if we can be diligent like the beaver." The more we know about and understand a character quality, the easier it is to apply it in everyday life.

- Each morning, remind your family members about the character quality of the month, and then you can look forward to hearing at supper how they applied that quality to situations throughout the day. This will also provide time and opportunities for you to explain how you are learning the character quality with them and how you have either seen the benefits of demonstrating it or the results of failing to apply it.

- To help children build a specific quality into their thinking process, have them write out the definition or draw a picture of the animal demonstrating the quality they need to work on. Older family members can write out the quality and definition on a card and put it on their mirror, in their car, or in their pocket. Those with a computer may be able to put it on their screen saver.

As parents get involved in the daily activities of their children, they will be able to encourage good character.

4 *Recognizing* good character

As we make decisions on a moment-by-moment basis, we are either demonstrating good character or a lack of good character. We can recognize specific qualities— or a lack of them—in our own lives by comparing our words, actions, and attitudes to the quality's definition. The definition of a character quality is like a yardstick. As we apply the quality to our lives, we can measure our behavior with this "yardstick" and determine what areas we need to work on.

5 *Correcting* for good character

Parents have the responsibility to correct and discipline their children. In order for correction to be effective, there must be a proper relationship already existing between parents and children. Proper relationships are developed when parents show true concern and genuine interest for their children.

Appropriate correction stems from love and not from anger. Parents must establish standards of behavior for their children, and character must be the basis of correction. The purpose of correction is to benefit the child and to restore the parent/child relationship that has been damaged through disobedience. Character-based correction teaches children that good character wins their parents' approval.

- In correcting children, parents must act immediately; however, correction must be in private. The disobedient child must learn personal responsibility by truthfully admitting what he or she did wrong. Parents can teach their children by asking them questions such as, "Were you truthful?" "Were you grateful?" "Was that compassionate?" Once children see how they were wrong, they can begin to apply good character. Proper correction involves a change of heart and a positive change in behavior rather than guilt or regret. The goal of correction is to mend a damaged relationship and channel the child toward good character for his or her benefit.

"Let me die in the advocacy of what is just and right."
Abraham Lincoln

Building a Character Family *step by step*

PHASE IV: PROCEDURE

1 **Gather the family together** for a special meeting.
   - The family will gauge how important character is by the priority you put on it.

2 **Explain the importance** of character to their success and what it means to be a Character Family.
   - Tell your family you want to spend more time with them and that you see needs in yourself and in the family that you want them all to work on together. Humble yourself before them if there are mistakes you need to clear up, as these must be taken care of before you can truly lead your Character Family. However, do not make any commitments you are not prepared to keep.

3 **Pass a Character Family resolution** and explain that this is a commitment to work on character as a family. Frame the resolution and hang it in a prominent place as a continual reminder to family members of their commitment.
   - Build this up as much as you want to. Children love pomp and circumstance, and many young people like it more than they may reveal. Make each one feel privileged to be a part of such a family.

4 **Share your plan:** Tell them you will focus on one character quality per month (or whatever pace you have predetermined). As a family, you will learn about the quality, memorize the definition, and look for ways to apply it every day around the house, at school, at work, and at play. Family members can then report back during the next family meeting about the ways they applied the quality and the rewards that came as a result.

Building a Character Family *week by week*

Schools, businesses, and families have found it most effective to focus on one character quality per month. Below are sample lesson plans for all four weeks of the month, which a Character Family can use in getting started. These ideas may be adapted for your family, and as you progress, your family "character initiative" will become unique and you will create your own ideas for building character together.

At dinner, ask the children how they have been able to apply the quality during the day.

Week One:

- Read the quality, definition, and "I will"s.
- Discuss the goal to demonstrate the quality as a family.
- Read about the animal and historical figure (where applicable).
- Have each family member explain what this quality means to him or her.
- Act out real-life situations that display the quality or a lack of it.
- Make a list of friends or family members who have displayed this quality.

- Young children may enjoy drawing or coloring the animal.

- Post the quality and definition in a prominent place.

Week Two:

- As a family, say the definition aloud.

- Recall from memory key points about the animal and historical figure.

- Read the applications for the home and the rewards.

- Discuss how these applications relate to your family.

- Discuss one specific way to improve as a family in the following week.

- Talk about the rewards, and anticipate their benefits in the week to come.

- Memorize the first two "I will"s.

- Memorize the definition of the character quality.

Week Three:

- Have each family member individually say the definition from memory.

- Read the third and fourth "I will"s.

- One by one, discuss ways that the "I will"s have or have not been applied.

- Have each person give a personal example of the rewards he or she experienced during the previous week.

- Write notes to one another expressing gratefulness for a specific way each family member has applied the quality.

Week Four:

- Review the definition from memory.

- Read the fifth "I will."

- Have each person tell how he or she can apply the "I will" for that week.

- Review memorization of all the "I will"s and the definition.

- As a family, choose memorable names or phrases to remind everyone to display the quality, such as "joyful as an otter" or "diligent as a beaver."

- Have a celebration of awards and rewards—Give each other special prizes that directly relate to the rewards of the quality.

These steps and helpful hints should prepare you to begin the adventure of *Achieving True Success* through building a Character Family. However, the best way to learn how to do it is to go ahead and just do it! Have fun as you launch out to . . .

Build Character as a Family

Turn menial tasks into opportunities to develop character qualities such as orderliness, thoroughness, and joyfulness.

To make birthdays more meaningful, have each family member praise the one with the birthday for a quality appreciated in him or her.

When young people see how specific character qualities will help them achieve their goals, they will be motivated to develop them.

As family members invest in each others' lives, relationships will be built and strengthened.

"It is only as we develop others that we permanently succeed."

Harvey S. Firestone

"Fame is a vapor,
Popularity an accident,
Riches take wing,
And only character endures."

Horace Greeley

"The greatest waste in the world is the difference
between what we are and what we could be."

John Grimes

Achieving True Success

How to Build Character as a Family

49 Qualities for Success

How to Build Character as a Family

This section is intended to be a resource for your family. It contains 49 key character qualities that are vital for true success. Each quality is amplified and illustrated to make it understandable and applicable to daily life. Most families, schools, and businesses find it helpful to focus on one quality per month.

The amplifications for each quality are explained below and correspond with the opposite page:

A The **character qualities** are arranged alphabetically throughout this section.

> Practical application: Introduce the quality during a family character meeting and remind the family of the quality throughout the month.

B The **opposite** of the quality helps to clarify its meaning.

> Practical application: Just as character qualities are linked to success, their opposites lead to failure. By pinpointing these opposites in their own lives, family members can identify the character qualities they need to give special attention to.

C The **definition** of a character quality is its most crucial component. These operational definitions are action-oriented, because it is not enough to *know* the right thing to do— we must *do* it.

> Practical application: Memorize the definition of the quality for the month. Creativity aides in memory work and could include placing plaques or posters of the definition around the house, hand motions to correspond with each word, and memory games.

D The **animal** kingdom displays a wealth of insight into good character.

> Practical application: Animal illustrations help to make abstract qualities more concrete. They are especially effective in teaching children.

E Until a quality is consistently demonstrated **in the home**, where our true selves tend to be most revealed, it has not yet been learned.

> Practical application: The applications for the home are suggestions for your family. They are designed to make the quality practical and to stimulate further ideas and discussion.

F As specific qualities are applied, specific **rewards** can be expected. Decisions based on good character are like seeds planted in the ground. It may be a matter of time, but good things will come. These are just a few specific rewards.

> Practical application: Ask your children if they want these rewards. Then teach them what is required to receive them. Anticipation of reward is excellent motivation.

G Developing character involves making a decision to apply a specific quality to everyday life. The **"I will" statements** break down a quality into practical commitments.

> Practical application: Say the "I will"s aloud with your family and help each other memorize them. When children disobey, point them back to these commitments they have made.

H **Heroes of character** give a historical perspective and remind us that the qualities demonstrated by these heroes have stood the test of time and have rewarded all who practiced them.

> Practical application: Read these short stories to the family. Do further research on these heroes and the ones you yourselves discover.

I **Quotes** are designed to convey conventional wisdom about the quality and to inspire noble thoughts and actions. **Beautiful illustrations** remind us that good character is truly beautiful.

> Practical application: Enjoy!

The ultimate goal of a Character Family . . .

Family Harmony

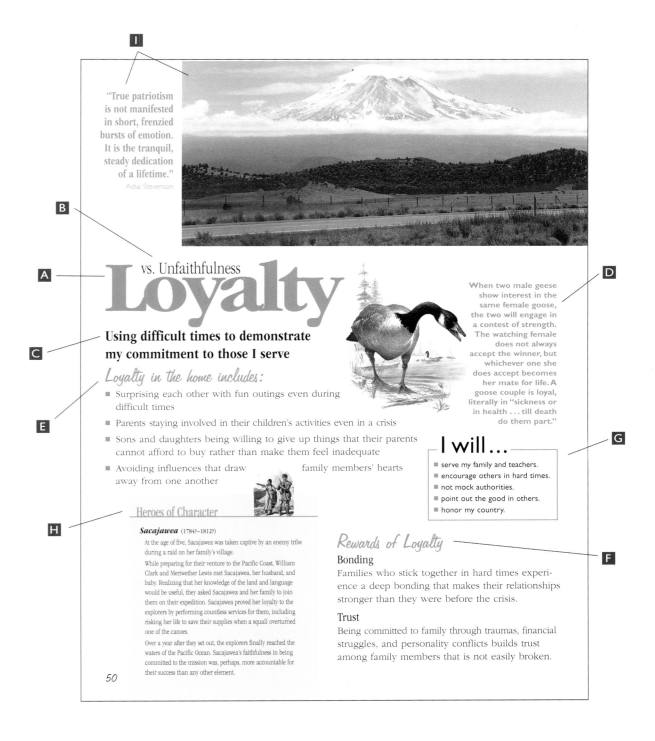

"True patriotism is not manifested in short, frenzied bursts of emotion. It is the tranquil, steady dedication of a lifetime."

Adlai Stevenson

vs. Unfaithfulness
Loyalty

Using difficult times to demonstrate my commitment to those I serve

Loyalty in the home includes:

- Surprising each other with fun outings even during difficult times
- Parents staying involved in their children's activities even in a crisis
- Sons and daughters being willing to give up things that their parents cannot afford to buy rather than make them feel inadequate
- Avoiding influences that draw family members' hearts away from one another

When two male geese show interest in the same female goose, the two will engage in a contest of strength. The watching female does not always accept the winner, but whichever one she does accept becomes her mate for life. A goose couple is loyal, literally in "sickness or in health . . . till death do them part."

I will...

- serve my family and teachers.
- encourage others in hard times.
- not mock authorities.
- point out the good in others.
- honor my country.

Heroes of Character

Sacajawea (1784?–1812?)

At the age of five, Sacajawea was taken captive by an enemy tribe during a raid on her family's village.

While preparing for their venture to the Pacific Coast, William Clark and Meriwether Lewis met Sacajawea, her husband, and baby. Realizing that her knowledge of the land and language would be useful, they asked Sacajawea and her family to join them on their expedition. Sacajawea proved her loyalty to the explorers by performing countless services for them, including risking her life to save their supplies when a squall overturned one of the canoes.

Over a year after they set out, the explorers finally reached the waters of the Pacific Ocean. Sacajawea's faithfulness in being committed to the mission was, perhaps, more accountable for their success than any other element.

50

Rewards of Loyalty

Bonding
Families who stick together in hard times experience a deep bonding that makes their relationships stronger than they were before the crisis.

Trust
Being committed to family through traumas, financial struggles, and personality conflicts builds trust among family members that is not easily broken.

49 Qualities for Success at a glance

Alertness *vs. Carelessness*

Being aware of what is taking place around me so I can have the right responses

The alert ring-necked pheasant anticipates the actions of predators and avoids the deadly effect of their attack. Surviving by wit and elusiveness, this bird continues to thrive and prosper largely due to its alertness.

Alertness in the home includes:

- Looking for and praising ways that family members have displayed good character

- Sensing that seemingly harmless activities could lead to bad influences and wrong friends

- Being aware that participation in certain activities and wearing certain clothing could attract the wrong friends and weaken the trust of authorities

- Practicing preventive maintenance with household appliances and personal health

I will...

- keep my eyes and ears open.
- listen for little things.
- heed warning signals.
- tell others of danger.
- stay away from unsafe places.

Rewards of Alertness

Safety
An alert family is able to see and avoid dangers.

Preparedness
An alert family is forewarned about situations and circumstances and is therefore able to prepare for them.

Attentiveness *vs. Distraction*

Showing the worth of a person or task by giving my undivided concentration

Attentiveness in the home includes:

- Showing support for each other by listening to another's ideas without immediately getting irritated or finding fault in them

- Encouraging other family members by expressing an interest in their activities

- Setting aside time to listen with eyes and ears to a family member's counsel and concerns

- Making family members feel important by spending time alone with each of them and listening to their interests

- Learning what each family member enjoys so that extra touches can be added to birthday celebrations and other special occasions

Rewards of Attentiveness

Respect
An attentive person gains the respect of others as they value his or her opinion the way he or she has valued theirs.

Key to knowledge
You will discover that the secret to learning is asking as many questions as you can and listening carefully to the answers.

There is more to the white-tailed deer's attentiveness than its acute hearing. The deer carefully evaluates the sights, sounds, and smells it receives. It is the mental processes behind the deer's senses that make it truly attentive.

I will...
- look at people when they speak to me.
- ask questions if I don't understand.
- sit or stand up straight.
- not draw attention to myself.
- keep my eyes, ears, hands, feet, and mouth from distractions.

"A good listener is not only popular everywhere, but after a while he knows something."

Wilson Mizner

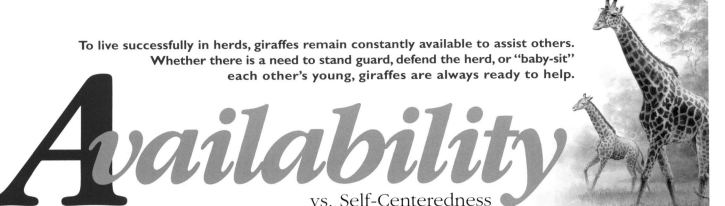

To live successfully in herds, giraffes remain constantly available to assist others. Whether there is a need to stand guard, defend the herd, or "baby-sit" each other's young, giraffes are always ready to help.

Availability

vs. Self-Centeredness

Making my own schedule and priorities secondary to the wishes of those I serve

Availability in the home includes:

- Family members doing what would please the other when spending time together
- Putting aside personal hobbies when they conflict with family time
- Stopping in the middle of a project to hear what another family member has to say
- Changing plans with friends in order to help the family prepare for guests

I will...

- put others ahead of myself.
- find a way to help, not a way to hide.
- be ready when I'm called.
- be glad for the chance to serve.
- check with the right person before I make commitments.

Rewards of Availability

Abundance
The success of those whom you help will spill back into your own life.

Stability
Families who place priority on each others' needs foster an atmosphere of peace in the home. This peace gives a family stability in hard times.

Heroes of Character

George Washington (1732–1799)

As a young man, George Washington's dream was to go into the Royal Navy. When he was fifteen he received a position on a ship, but his mother pleaded with him not to go. Heeding his mother's wishes, George gave up his dream of being a sailor and took a position as a surveyor while tending to the needs of his widowed mother.

In the middle of his career, George's brother Lawrence had to go to Barbados to recover from illness, and he urged George to go with him. Although it conflicted with his own plans, George accompanied his brother, falling ill with smallpox himself while there.

Learning availability at a young age prepared George Washington for the decisions he would face later in his life when he was asked to lead the Continental Army and afterward, the United States. Although he would have preferred home life at Mount Vernon, he answered the call of duty and led the colonies to victory in the American Revolution, earning the title "The Father of His Country."

"He gives too late who waits to be asked."
Latin proverb

Benevolence in the home includes:

- Treating each family member with the same respect shown to those outside the family

- Choosing to look upon mundane household duties, such as doing laundry and cooking meals, as a labor of love for the family

- Caring about another family member's growth in character more than his or her material achievements

- Focusing on each other's inner needs and desires rather than selfishly seeking one's own success by fulfilling personal ambitions

I will...

- look for people in need.
- treat others how I want to be treated.
- give food, clothing, and shelter.
- be patient with others.
- give more as I get more.

Benevolence
vs. Selfishness

Giving to others' basic needs without having as my motive personal reward

Rewards of Benevolence

Favor
Unselfishly caring about others opens the doors to their hearts.

Peace and safety
Selfishness is conquered when people truly care about each other. When a person seeks the good of others, he or she desires to protect, rather than harm, their bodies and emotions.

After an emperor penguin mother lays an egg, the father lifts the egg off the cold Antarctic ice onto his feet and snuggles it beneath his warm belly. For longer than three months, the father stands still, making a significant sacrifice of personal freedom for the benefit of his young.

Boldness
vs. Fearfulness

CONFIDENCE that what I have to say or do is true, right, and just

Boldness in the home includes:

- Consistently living out the character standards the family has set for themselves, even if others do not understand

- Being ready to explain to those outside the family the family's commitment to good character

- Going to one another in a loving spirit when he or she is not demonstrating good character

- Not being afraid to walk away from friends who are engaged in foolish or harmful activities

I will...

- not be afraid to speak the truth.
- keep a clear conscience.
- support others when they are right.
- be willing to stand alone.
- speak with humility.

> "A bold man is better in all things."
>
> Homer's *Odyssey*

LEARN HOW ONE MAN GAINED
Power Over Fear

A man was diagnosed with cancer and was told he had only a few months to live. Soon after that, a burglar was trapped in a nearby store. The man volunteered to go in and apprehend the criminal. He reasoned that if he died in the process, he would become a hero rather than experience an uneventful death. The burglar was so overwhelmed by this man's boldness that he surrendered.

The man volunteered for other acts of bravery and astonished everyone. But then the doctors informed him that they had misdiagnosed his case. He did not have cancer and would live. His fear returned, and his courage and power were lost.

for example

Reward of Boldness
Safety

Fear of what others think may cause a person to lower his or her own standards of good conduct to please them. As a result, this person could be easily deceived and trapped by others. A bold person will keep himself or herself safe from dangerous people.

"Look before you leap."
Unknown

Cautiousness in the home includes:

- Deciding if the family has enough money for major expenditures—before making them

- Foreseeing negative influences in a seemingly good opportunity and avoiding them

- Seeking counsel from one another before finalizing decisions

- Judging an activity by whether or not it would encourage good character

- Asking the owner's permission before taking or moving his or her belongings

Rewards of Cautiousness

Foundation
The family unit will continue to be rooted in strength and commitment as wise precautions are taken.

Peace
Visualizing undesirable consequences of activities that could possibly be hurtful gives assurance and peace in one's wise decisions.

Decisiveness
Families have a greater ability to be decisive when precautions are carefully considered and evaluated.

I will...
- think before I act.
- follow safety rules.
- ask permission.
- talk at the right time.
- look out for danger.

Living in the vast, open regions of the plains, a prairie dog cannot be too careful. Because the prairie dog is the choice meal of numerous predators, cautiousness is built into its habits.

vs. Rashness

Cautiousness

Knowing how IMPORTANT right timing is in accomplishing right actions

Compassion vs. Indifference

Investing whatever is necessary to heal the hurts of others

Unable to keep up with the herd, sick or injured zebras become easy prey to their chasing attackers. Instead of leaving them behind to face certain destruction, the rest of the herd slows down enough for everyone to stay together. With a little sacrifice from others, the hurting members are given a chance to recover from their wounds.

Compassion in the home includes:

- Realizing each other's needs for love and attention, and planning outings and activities to meet those needs

- Sensing each other's need for respect and listening to ideas with an open mind

- Seeking to understand another's struggles from his or her viewpoint and experiences

- Being willing to give up activities that could disappoint and hurt one another

Rewards of Compassion

Favor

A person who diligently seeks the good of another will receive approval and favor of those who observe their unselfish actions.

Friendship

Becoming involved in the life of another brings a deeper level of intimacy and friendship.

I will...

- stop to help.
- listen when others want to talk.
- give of my resources to help those in need.
- look for lasting solutions.
- comfort others without regard to race, gender, faith, age, or nationality.

"The friend [in] my adversity I shall always cherish most. I can better trust those who helped to relieve the gloom of my dark hours than those who are so ready to enjoy with me the sunshine of my prosperity."

Ulysses S. Grant

"To the contented, even poverty is joy. To the discontented, even wealth is a vexation."

Chinese proverb

Contentment vs. Covetousness

Realizing that true happiness does not depend on material conditions

Contentment in the home includes:

- Focusing on building family relationships by spending time together at home instead of always seeking extravagant means of entertainment with friends

- Parents investing time in the children instead of using money to win their favor

- Being willing to buy less in order to stay within the family budget

- Learning to have fewer things and enjoy them more

- Avoiding the temptations of advertisements, window-shopping, and catalogs when those purchases are unnecessary

Reward of Contentment
Health

Envy makes a person dissatisfied with his or her own family, abilities, and possessions so much so that it acts like a parasite, eating away at the heart and causing the bones to rot.

I will...

- be thankful for what I have.
- not complain about what I don't have.
- value people more than things.
- take care of my belongings.
- not be jealous of others.

The deer mouse is content in just about any location. It may set up house in an abandoned squirrel's nest inside a tree, in an old bird's nest on the outside of a tree, under old stumps and logs, or in stone walls, cliffs, caves, or buildings.

> "The significant problems we face today cannot be solved at the same level of thinking we were at when we created them."
>
> Albert Einstein

CREATIVITY

vs. Underachievement

Approaching a need, a task, or an idea

from a new perspective

Creativity in the home includes:

- Discovering ways to make household chores fun, such as playing music while working or going out for a treat after the work is done

- Starting traditions, creating new games, and finding new places to go on birthdays, vacations, and holidays

- Learning to make your own unique thank-you cards

- Turning homework into learning games and putting memory work to music

Rewards of Creativity

Good memories

Turning special holidays, as well as the mundane days, into fun adventures will create stories to talk and laugh about for years.

Achievement

Accomplishing necessary work in creative and unique ways brings a great sense of achievement.

I will...

- try new things.
- ask for help.
- remember what worked in the past.
- study to solve problems.
- use my talents for good.

Perhaps no animal is as curious and creative as the raccoon. Raccoons have been known to figure out how to open the latches on doors in order to get into a farmer's outbuildings.

The badger is a tenacious creature. In a conflict, it is quick to decide whether or not to stand its ground, and then it wholeheartedly pursues its decision.

Decisiveness in the home includes:

- Firmly establishing the family commitment to good character by forming habits based on desired qualities

- Discussing with each other the decisions that need to be finalized to avoid making rash choices based on the impulse of the moment

- Making decisions based on a commitment to character vs. popular opinion

- Keeping each other accountable to not procrastinate

Rewards of Decisiveness

Success

Obtaining wise counsel from many before finalizing a decision will ensure its success.

Confidence

Procrastination of decision making often results in confusion and wasted time; when families base decisions on previous commitments, they will have greater confidence in their decisions.

I will...

- make wise decisions.
- get good counsel.
- consider the positives and negatives.
- decide things promptly.
- not worry.

DECISIVENESS
vs. Procrastination

The ability to recognize key factors and finalize difficult decisions

"Decide not rashly. The decision made can never be recalled."

Longfellow

Deference in the home includes:

- Speaking with clean language to other members of the family

- Dressing modestly in the home so as not to offend

- Refraining from wrong activities in order to be role models for younger family members

- Showing respect to parents by not talking back or using ugly words

Deference vs. Rudeness

Limiting my freedom so I do not offend the tastes of those around me

I will...

- notice those around me.
- respect the feelings of others.
- not use offensive language.
- not play loud music in public.
- be careful how I dress.

Rewards of Deference

Respect
People respect those who are willing to give up questionable activities in order to avoid offending others.

Good name
The person who limits his or her freedom in deference to another builds a good name that others will praise.

"Every action in company ought to be with some sign of respect to those present."

George Washington

30

Dependability vs. Inconsistency

Fulfilling what I consented to do, even if it means unexpected sacrifice

"It is easier to do a job right than to explain why you didn't."
— Martin Van Buren

Dependability in the home includes:

- Committing to stay together even through financial difficulties and personality conflicts
- Parents being faithful to go to work and provide for the family
- Sons and daughters completing their homework every day
- Helping family members to avoid making commitments they cannot keep
- Family members fulfilling promises they make to each other

Rewards of Dependability

Praise
When family members are reliable, they receive praise from each other at home as well as in public.

Responsibility
Children who prove to be dependable in little things will gain the trust of their parents. Their parents will in turn trust them in more significant areas and give added responsibility.

I will...
- keep my word.
- be careful what I promise.
- correct my mistakes.
- pull my share of the load.
- not have a bad attitude.

The tank-like build of the musk ox is an ominous warning to any would-be attacker. But young musk oxen are not so imposing. The smaller oxen depend on the adults in the herd to stand between them and dangerous wolves.

I will...

- set goals.
- make sure my goals are right.
- ignore distractions.
- not be discouraged by others.
- face problems head-on.

Determination in the home includes:

- Parents telling their children stories from their own lives of how sticking with a task led to success

- Pursuing excellence in the appearance and harmony of the home, while avoiding the trap of perfectionism

- Refusing to let the latest trends dictate how the family functions

- Young people focusing on their parents' vision for the family without allowing the opinions of others to disillusion them

"Genius is 2 percent inspiration, 98 percent perspiration."

Thomas Edison

vs. Faintheartedness

DETERMINATION

Purposing to accomplish right goals at the right time, regardless of the opposition

Rewards of Determination

Courage
Facing fierce winds and storms with an undaunted attitude builds a strong, protective layer called courage.

Satisfaction
Few things are more rewarding than the exhilaration of achievement after wholehearted effort. The harder the fight, the sweeter the victory.

After one to four years at sea, the king salmon determines to head home—back to the stream where it hatched. Swimming against the fierce river currents and leaping up waterfalls, the mighty salmon actually increases its daily speed as it covers the hundreds of miles home.

vs. Slothfulness
DILIGENCE
Investing my time and energy to complete each task assigned to me

Diligence in the home includes:

- Parents investing time and energy to establish vision and goals for the family

- Helping to plan and set priorities for weekly tasks for the family to accomplish

- Making a daily schedule to use time most wisely

- Putting just as much effort into helping family members with their responsibilities as is put into one's own responsibilities

The phrase "busy as a beaver" is a tribute to the diligence that makes beavers successful. Rarely is a beaver inactive. It is constantly building, maintaining, working ahead, and caring for its family. Even after their own dam and lodge are established, parent beavers will keep busy by building additional dams and lodges for future generations.

Heroes of Character

Benjamin Oliver Davis (1877–1970)

Benjamin Oliver Davis was born into a legacy of diligence. His grandfather was a slave who bought his freedom through hard work. His father was a servant for General John A. Logan, who was so impressed with his work that he helped him secure a position as a messenger for the Department of the Interior.

After graduating from Howard University, Benjamin enlisted in the U.S. Army and was soon promoted to sergeant-major and then to second lieutenant for his exemplary service. As professor of military science and tactics at Wilberforce University and the Tuskegee Institute, he was highly respected by the cadets in his charge and known for his emphasis on firm discipline. After serving in the Philippines during World War I, he acted as an advisor to General Dwight Eisenhower during World War II.

In 1940, after 42 years of diligent and faithful service in the Army, Benjamin O. Davis became the first black general in the U.S. Army when he was promoted to brigadier general. The legacy lived on in his own son, Benjamin Oliver Davis Jr., who earned 39 medals for his heroism and outstanding service to his country and attained the rank of lieutenant general, the second highest rank in the U.S. Military.

Rewards of Diligence

Direction

Diligent people have vision for their lives; they use every available moment and opportunity to accomplish goals. Unlike a lazy person who is constantly "wading through molasses," a diligent person sees his or her way clearly without confusion.

Promotion

A person who is diligent with his or her skills and talents will not lack opportunities and sought-after positions.

I will...

- finish my projects.
- do a job right.
- follow instructions.
- concentrate on my work.
- not be lazy.

"Small deeds done are better than great deeds planned."

General George C. Marshall

Discernment
vs. Shortsightedness

Understanding the DEEPER reasons why things happen

Discernment in the home includes:

- Perceiving that selfishness leads to a breakdown in relationships

- Realizing that rebellion in children may come from an unmet need for parental approval and acceptance

- Knowing when it is wise to pay a large sum for an item

- Understanding that addictions, wrong friends, suicide, and violence can be caused by unresolved bitterness, guilt, and lack of purpose in life

The bobcat patiently stalks and watches its intended prey, discerning its movements, its path, and the best direction from which to approach. The bobcat knows it has only one chance, so it waits until what it discerns to be the best opportunity to leap from its cover and strike.

Rewards of Discernment

Discretion
Understanding the root causes of a family crisis will enable families to have the foresight to avoid wrong attitudes and actions in the future.

Peace
Focusing on building good character and meeting the needs of each other brings peace instead of conflict.

I will...

- ask questions.
- not judge hastily.
- learn from experience.
- not repeat mistakes.
- trace problems to their causes.

"We sometimes see a fool possessed of wit, but never of judgment."
La Rochefoucauld

34

> "I have never been hurt by anything I didn't say."
>
> Calvin Coolidge

I will...

- choose my words carefully.
- practice good manners.
- not make fun of others.
- consider the consequences.
- stay away from trouble.

Discretion in the home includes:

- Being careful to not say things that could spark a fight or argument
- Keeping the wrong influences from certain movies and books out of the home
- Refraining from the use of words that could discourage one another
- Helping one another remember to think before speaking
- Avoiding negative body language and words that criticize and dishonor one another
- Foreseeing the hidden extra costs of spending more than the family income

The cleverness for which the red fox is known is largely due to its discretion. When pursued, the fox constantly evaluates its direction and makes strategic changes to avoid giving itself away by its trail, its noise, or being sighted.

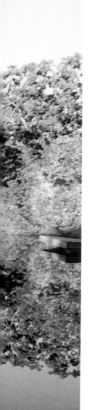

Discretion
vs. Simplemindedness

Recognizing and avoiding words, actions, and attitudes that could bring UNDESIRABLE consequences

Rewards of Discretion

Friendship

Gossip can cause strife between even the best of friends. Refusing to speak negatively of another person behind his or her back gives the opportunity for deep, unbroken friendships.

Safety

Having the prudence to know when a pathway may be dangerous and choosing to avoid it ensures safety from ugly scars and hurt.

Endurance vs. Discouragement

The inward strength to withstand stress and do my *best*

Endurance in the home includes:

- Facing up to financial debt with the persistence to pay it off
- Parents having the faith not to give up hope for a disobedient child
- Sticking to the task with homework, housework, and family projects
- Bearing each others' burdens and hanging in there together

For centuries, the camel has served as a reliable source of transportation across areas impassable by any other means. From its nose to its tail, the camel is uniquely designed to withstand the stress of harsh desert conditions that stops most creatures dead in their tracks.

Rewards of Endurance

Opportunities

Continuing to do what is right even through hard times will lead a person to unexpected opportunities that would have been missed if he or she had quit.

Strength

The willingness to learn from hard times and difficult relationships builds strength of character that makes it worth it all.

I will...

- not give up.
- keep my eyes on the goal.
- take one step at a time.
- not let criticism discourage me.
- keep going even though I am tired.

Heroes of Character

Mary McLeod Bethune (1875–1955)

As the fifteenth of seventeen children born to former slaves, Sam and Patsy McLeod, Mary McLeod worked alongside her family as they struggled to make a living planting cotton in a small field they bought from their former owner.

When Mary was eleven, her parents heard of a school for girls that she could attend. Wanting at least one of their children to get an education, they sent Mary, the first of their children to be born free, to school. Through her diligent study, she received a scholarship to a college and graduated at the age of twenty.

Grateful for the opportunity she had received to get an education, she decided to open a girls' school so she could share her learning with others. With $1.50 and five students, the Daytona Literary and Industrial School for Training Negro Girls was born. Although many people objected and tried to close it down, Mary Bethune refused to be intimidated. What started with one woman who was determined to teach five girls how to read, eventually became Bethune-Cookman College. Mary Bethune personally worked with many presidents, and in June of 1936 was appointed director of the Division of Negro Affairs and became the first black woman to serve as the head of a federal agency.

Enthusiasm

A Part of zeal

vs. Apathy

Expressing joy in each task as I give it my _best_ effort

Enthusiasm in the home includes:

- Showing excitement about lessons learned through life struggles
- Completing chores in good time with a positive attitude motivated by a love for making things clean and shiny
- Tackling work with a vision of how it will benefit others
- Showing genuine interest in the games and activities that other family members enjoy

I will...

- be an energy-giver.
- smile.
- treat every job as important.
- put my whole heart into what I do.
- not be discouraged by failure.

Rewards of Enthusiasm

Renewal

Showing genuine interest in every task provides a person with a renewed excitement about life.

Strong bones

Not only does enthusiasm brighten the face and give light to the eyes, but it also acts as a natural medicine that builds strong and thick bones.

At 50 feet long and weighing 50 tons, the humpback whale cannot help but do things in a big way. This songster of the ocean sings tunes that often last 20 minutes and resonate through the water for hundreds of miles.

"Nothing great was ever achieved without enthusiasm."

Ralph Waldo Emerson

37

Faith vs. Presumption

Confidence that actions rooted in good character will yield the best outcome, even when I cannot see how

Squirrels cannot fly, but that does not stop these little rodents from taking a "leap of faith." Equipped with folds of skin that extend between their outstretched legs like wings, flying squirrels gracefully glide between lofty branches.

Faith in the home includes:

- Avoiding expenses that would exceed the family income, even when the family cannot see how their needs will be met

- Visualizing achievement for each family member and helping him or her live up to his or her full potential

- Sons and daughters trusting their parents' leadership and counsel even though it may not make sense to them now

- Believing the best about each other and giving each other the benefit of the doubt

- Being willing to give up friends and activities that violate good character, even when no other friends are available

Rewards of Faith

Decisiveness

Faith gives a person the confidence to take the first step, knowing that the next step will then become clear.

Good things

Faith enables a person to give up what seems good on the surface and patiently wait for what he or she knows is best. "Good things come to those who wait."

I will...

- rely on good principles.
- not take things for granted.
- trust those with proven character.
- hope for the best.
- not worry about the future.

Flexibility in the home includes:

- Being willing to change ideas or plans based on the cautions of one another

- Being open to one another's suggestions on how to improve home life

- Welcoming family emergencies as opportunities to build character

- Giving up activities that conflict with family priorities—without griping

Rewards of Flexibility

Insight

The willingness to change one's ideas or plans in favor of another's gives new insight into activities or perspectives not yet explored.

Success

Resisting the good advice of others may lead to wrong decisions. If one is willing to change his or her plans in response to good advice, success will result from wise decisions.

Flexibility vs. Resistance

Willingness to change plans or ideas according to the direction of my authorities

Hummingbirds demonstrate amazing flexibility. These agile, three-and-a-half-inch birds dart between and hover over flowers to drink nectar, and they ably catch insects in flight. The hummingbird's well-developed wing muscles account for 25 to 30 percent of its total body weight.

I will...

- not get upset when plans change.
- respect the decisions of my authorities.
- not be stubborn.
- look for the good in changes.
- not compromise what is right.

"If you want to grow, you must be willing to stretch."

Anonymous

Forgiveness
VS. REJECTION

Clearing the record of those who have wronged me and not holding a grudge

I will...

- be quick to forgive.
- not cover up my own wrongs but will be quick to ask for forgiveness.
- not seek revenge.
- respond kindly to those who hurt me.
- not take up offenses for others.

"A wise man will make haste to forgive, because he knows the true value of time, and will not suffer it to pass away in unnecessary pain."

Samuel Johnson

A shepherd is responsible to care for and protect his sheep. Sheep are dependent animals and must be shown what to eat, where to drink, and where to rest. They must also be protected from predators. Many times this task is difficult, because sheep are prone to wander and stray from the flock.

Forgiveness in the home includes:

- Discussing personal differences in order to learn more about each other's needs
- A parent disciplining a disobedient child in love and not in anger
- Talking with each other about hurts instead of stuffing it down inside
- Responding to another's rude words with a kind tone of voice

Rewards of Forgiveness

Friendship

Forgetting the hurtful words and actions of another by focusing on that person's strong points will allow friendships to blossom.

Love

People who ask forgiveness for the wrong they have done will experience the love that comes from a deepened relationship.

40

The pelican is so well equipped to catch fish that it catches enough for itself and others. Though other birds steal fish right out of the pelican's mouth, the pelican never complains or seeks revenge.

Generosity in the home includes:

- Helping one another on projects he or she cannot finish alone
- Refraining from spending too much money on things that would not benefit the entire family
- Parents refraining from giving in to their children's every desire in order to have money and time to give them what they need
- Completing homework on time in order to help the family with chores and meals
- Giving up some personal free time to do activities with other family members

Generosity
VS. STINGINESS (OR possessiveness)

Carefully managing my resources so I can freely give to those in need

Rewards of Generosity

Joy
The paradox of generosity is that the more a person gives away, the happier he or she becomes. Giving brings even more happiness than receiving.

Friendship
Far more important than even the tangible benefits given to others is the relationship that develops between giver and recipient. No amount of sacrifice can outweigh the value of a vibrant friendship with another person.

I will...
- share what I have with others.
- recycle.
- not expect anything in return for my generosity.
- give of my time and talents.
- praise the good I see in others.

"One cannot be too generous. Very few try; and none succeed."
Percival Christopher Wren

Eastern bluebirds make their homes in the fence posts and tree stumps of the central and eastern United States. Their beautiful songs, provision of food for their young, and commitment of time and attention to the incubation of eggs demonstrate the gentleness of the parents toward their families.

Gentleness in the home includes:

- Respecting one another's need for occasional peace and quiet
- Being careful to tread lightly when another is hurting
- Choosing to not make jokes about one another
- Turning off loud music, television programs, or movies when they disturb others

Gentleness
vs. Harshness

Showing consideration and personal concern for others

I will...
- speak kindly to others.
- use a soft voice.
- open doors to let others go first.
- try not to break things.
- not be annoyed by others.

Rewards of Gentleness

Gladness
A kind word lifts heavy hearts and brings joy to the giver as well as to the receiver. It doesn't take much to brighten someone's day.

Calmness
Avoiding harsh words and inconsiderate actions prevents wounded spirits and walls between family members. A peaceful home is a rare and precious treasure, and gentleness greatly contributes to peace.

"Gentleness is able to accomplish what violence cannot."

Claudian

Heroes of Character

Roberto Clemente (1934–1972)

Growing up in Puerto Rico as the son of a sugarcane farmer, Roberto Clemente experienced first-hand the lifestyles and difficulties of those living in poverty, and he was determined to help them.

After being drafted by the Pittsburgh Pirates, he began using his influence to help establish medical clinics for the people of Latin America. For 17 years, he would return to his native land during the off-season to coach teams of young boys at a baseball camp he had set up for them.

When an earthquake in Nicaragua killed more than 6,000 people on Christmas Eve of 1972, he gathered food, clothing, and medicine to take to the victims. He was so concerned for the survivors that he decided to personally deliver the relief supplies and was killed when his plane crashed on the way to Nicaragua. Roberto showed the ultimate consideration and personal concern for others when he gave his life to meet their needs.

Gratefulness in the home includes:

- Doing menial tasks for family members so they do not have to do these tasks themselves

- Parents often telling their children that they believe in them and are glad they are part of their lives

- Saying "thank you" for the meal a parent worked to prepare

- Remembering and planning for each other's birthdays in order to make that one feel appreciated and loved

- Showing appreciation by doing things that are important to one another

I will...

- show my parents and teachers that I appreciate them.
- write "thank you" notes.
- take care of my things.
- be content with what I have.
- count my benefits rather than my burdens.

Rewards of Gratefulness

Joy
Discouragement is the consequence of overlooking or forgetting the many ways others have benefited our lives.

Friendship
Genuine love is built on a mutual understanding of our need for and appreciation of others.

The porcupine is a passive animal that means no harm to other creatures in the forest. However, it is equipped with a very effective defense system, without which it would not survive. Young porcupines, called porcupettes, learn to use their 33,000 needle-like quills to protect themselves. The porcupine has very poor eyesight but is content with its extra-special abilities.

Gratefulness vs. Unthankfulness

Letting others know by my words and actions how they have benefited my life

"To be capable of respect is almost as rare as to be worthy of it."

Joseph Joubert

vs. Disrespect
HONOR

Respecting others because of the HIGHER authorities they represent

Large herds of 3,000-pound Great Plains bison roamed the early American frontier by the thousands, led by elder bulls or cows. When the leading bison would move to a new feeding area, those nearest would follow. Other bison too distant to see the leader would follow those bison that could.

Honor in the home includes:

- Speaking positively about parents, employers, government officials, and law enforcement officers

- Showing respect to authorities by standing tall, making eye contact, addressing them with the correct titles, and having good manners

- Sons and daughters showing their parents esteem by calling home when they are out later than expected, asking permission to do things, making eye contact, and avoiding mumbling and slouching

Rewards of Honor

Honor
Showing honor to an authority will grab his or her attention. He or she will take an interest in the life of this respectful subordinate and will delight to give honor, as well as added responsibility in return.

Praise
Conducting oneself with good manners will cause others to take note; those in higher positions of authority will praise this person to others.

I will...
- respect my leaders.
- treat everyone with dignity.
- use good manners.
- not be sarcastic.
- remember that "all men are created equal."

vs. Loneliness

HOSPITALITY

Cheerfully sharing food, shelter, or conversation to BENEFIT others

The bighorn sheep of western America live in caves and on the slopes of the mountains. There, each member of the flock must hospitably share with others and look out for each other's safety.

Hospitality in the home includes:

- Being friendly to others by talking with neighbors, meeting new people, and greeting strangers with a smile
- Preparing for guests by organizing and cleaning the home and preparing meals
- Daily practicing both good etiquette and conversational skills to use with guests
- Diligently keeping the house free of clutter to make the home available and ready for unexpected guests

Rewards of Hospitality

Influence

Those whom you bring into your home to share a meal will be significantly influenced by your genuine care for them.

Role models

A big impact on your children's lives is made by the wise, older people who are invited to your home as they share stories of character in action from their own lives.

Heroes of Character

Dolly Madison (1768–1849)

When Dolly Madison was fifteen, her father suffered a financial reverse after freeing the family's slaves. As a result, she had to discontinue her schooling to take over the cooking chores and other assignments previously done by servants. She also became responsible for making clothes for her six younger brothers and sisters.

The skills she developed under these circumstances enabled her to be sensitive to the needs of others during the time she served as White House hostess, when her husband was Secretary of State under the widowed President Jefferson.

During her sixteen years as First Lady, Dolly Madison's social graces made her famous, and her polite tact maneuvered conversations to avoid conflicts. After the White House was burned by the British during the War of 1812, she continued to entertain even in temporary quarters. "It would be absolutely impossible for any-one to behave with more perfect propriety than she did," a resident of Washington wrote of her hostessing skills. She continued to practice hospitality in Washington until the time of her death.

"To have a friend, be a friend."

Common saying

Humility in the home includes:

- Praising each other for advice that enabled good decisions and the help that made achievements possible
- Showing gratefulness to the people who have invested time and effort to make one successful
- Sons and daughters recognizing the sacrifices of money, time, and energy their parents have made to help them succeed

Humility

VS. PRIDE

Acknowledging that achievement results from the investment of others in my life

The turkey vulture is not particularly attractive, intelligent, or agile. Yet this bird has saved more lives than perhaps any other creature. By devouring the remains of the dead, the turkey vulture stops the spread of disease and protects the lives of others.

WHAT HAPPENS WHEN YOU
Try to Do the Job Alone

The price of a lack of humility can be painful, as demonstrated in the following accident report:

"I am writing in response to your request that I explain in more detail what I meant by the cause of my accident, as I simply wrote 'Trying to do the job alone.'

"I am a bricklayer by trade. At the end of my work on the roof of a six-story building, I had about 500 lbs. of bricks left over. Rather than ask someone to help me, I decided to lower the bricks in a barrel using a pulley. After loading the bricks into the barrel, I went back to the ground and untied the rope, holding it tightly to assure a slow descent of the 500 lbs. of brick. Now you will notice above on the accident report that I weigh 135 lbs. In my surprise at being jerked off the ground, I lost my presence of mind and forgot to let go of the rope. Needless to say, I proceeded at a rather rapid rate up the side of the building. In the vicinity of the third floor, I met the barrel coming down, which explains the fractured skull and broken collarbone. I continued upward until the fingers of my right hand were two knuckles deep into the pulley.

"By this time I had regained my presence of mind and was able to hold tightly to the rope in spite of my pain. At about the same time, however, the barrel of bricks hit the ground and the bottom fell out, changing its weight to about 50 lbs. I refer you again to my weight mentioned above.

"As you might imagine, I began a rather rapid descent down the side of the building. In the vicinity of the third floor, I again met the barrel coming up. This accounts for the two broken ankles and the lacerations of my lower body. The encounter with the barrel slowed me enough to lessen my injuries when I fell onto the pile of bricks, and fortunately, only three vertebrae were cracked.

"I am sorry to report, however, that as I lay there on the bricks, in pain, unable to stand and watching the empty barrel six stories above me, I again lost my presence of mind, and I let go of the rope. The empty barrel weighed more than the rope, and it came down on me and broke both of my legs.

"I hope that I have furnished enough information about the accident, because, you see, I was trying to do the job alone."

for example

Rewards of Humility

Wisdom
Deeper levels of wisdom are gained when a person realizes that many people were involved in his or her accomplishments.

Honor
It is a joy to honor someone who is not always clamoring for the spotlight but instead shares the credit with others. Authorities love to exalt a humble person.

I will...

- remember what others have done for me.
- not boast or brag.
- serve without being recognized.
- pass on praise to others.
- never be "too high" for a job.

Initiative

VS. IDLENESS

Recognizing and doing what needs to be done before I am asked to do it

Initiative in the home includes:

- Accepting the challenge of being an example for other families and looking for ways to encourage them by sharing about lessons learned

- Parents visualizing achievement for each of their children and planning ahead for training opportunities that would help them reach their goals

- Seeing and doing chores around the house that need to be completed

Rewards of Initiative

Wealth

Faithfulness to daily plan and execute work is like putting a penny in a piggy bank every day. Little by little the pennies multiply, and one day they can make one rich.

Children's inheritance

Parents who take the initiative to plan and prepare for their children will have an inheritance to give to them.

I will...

- think ahead.
- look for ways to help others.
- volunteer.
- make the whole team successful.
- lead by example.

"A job well begun is half done."

Proverb

"Joy is the life of man's life."
Benjamin Whichcote

Joyfulness
vs. Self-Pity

Maintaining a GOOD ATTITUDE, even when faced with unpleasant conditions

I will...

- look for good in every situation.
- hope for the best.
- encourage others.
- smile and laugh.
- keep my mind on others instead of myself.

Joyfulness in the home includes:

- Remaining positive even when the family situation is not ideal or things are not going according to plan
- Smiling and speaking kindly to family members even when they forget to do what was asked of them
- Finding ways to solve family problems positively
- Cheerfully praising one another instead of blaming
- Greeting each other each morning with a cheerful smile
- Keeping the home bright with uplifting music

Rewards of Joyfulness

Strength

There is a special strength that emanates from a joyful person. This not only benefits that person's own life but also causes him or her to be an energy-giver to all those around.

Health

Medical research has confirmed that a joyful smile actually strengthens the immune system, which fights against disease in the body.

Newborn otters are afraid of water. The otter parents must gradually acquaint their young with the water by leading them near it, splashing in it, and eventually carrying them into a stream or lake. Soon the young otters discover that the experience they dreaded has become their greatest source of joy and provision.

I will...

- speak up for what is right.
- obey both the intent and letter of the law.
- deal with problems quickly.
- not accept bribes.
- hold myself to the same standards of right and wrong.

Justice
vs. Corruption

Taking **PERSONAL RESPONSIBILITY** to uphold what is pure, right, and true

"Justice, sir, is the great interest of man on earth."
Daniel Webster

Justice in the home includes:

- Setting a high standard for oneself in pure thoughts, right actions, and being loyal to the family

- Parents not only disciplining children for wrong decisions but training them to make right decisions

- Being responsible to protect one another from what is not pure or healthful

- Sharing belongings with one another, realizing that everything owned was once received

The bull African elephant upholds the social structure and prevents young males from forming gangs and harassing animals and people. He establishes a clear chain of command so that each individual has a safe and secure niche in the herd.

Rewards of Justice

Family stability

Corruption cannot destroy a family when each member is accountable to his or her own conscience to do what is right.

Secure society

When lawbreakers are swiftly and decisively punished, it is a great deterrent to crime. Children can then grow up in a secure environment without their parents being concerned for their safety.

49

Loyalty
vs. Unfaithfulness

Using difficult times to demonstrate my commitment to those I serve

Loyalty in the home includes:

- Surprising each other with fun outings even during difficult times

- Parents staying involved in their children's activities even in a crisis

- Sons and daughters being willing to give up things that their parents cannot afford to buy rather than make them feel inadequate

- Avoiding influences that draw family members' hearts away from one another

When two male geese show interest in the same female goose, the two will engage in a contest of strength. The watching female does not always accept the winner, but whichever one she does accept becomes her mate for life. A goose couple is loyal, literally in "sickness or in health . . . till death do them part."

I will...

- serve my family and teachers.
- encourage others in hard times.
- not mock authorities.
- point out the good in others.
- honor my country.

Heroes of Character

Sacajawea (1784?–1812?)

At the age of five, Sacajawea was taken captive by an enemy tribe during a raid on her family's village.

While preparing for their venture to the Pacific Coast, William Clark and Meriwether Lewis met Sacajawea, her husband, and baby. Realizing that her knowledge of the land and language would be useful, they asked Sacajawea and her family to join them on their expedition. Sacajawea proved her loyalty to the explorers by performing countless services for them, including risking her life to save their supplies when a squall overturned one of the canoes.

Over a year after they set out, the explorers finally reached the waters of the Pacific Ocean. Sacajawea's faithfulness in being committed to the mission was, perhaps, more accountable for their success than any other element.

Rewards of Loyalty

Bonding
Families who stick together in hard times experience a deep bonding that makes their relationships stronger than they were before the crisis.

Trust
Being committed to family through traumas, financial struggles, and personality conflicts builds trust among family members that is not easily broken.

50

For thousands of years, horses have been admired for their strength and beauty. The skill of training a horse begins with having the horse submit its will—without breaking its spirit.

Meekness vs. Anger

Yielding my personal rights and expectations, with a desire to serve

Meekness in the home includes:

- Family members yielding their rights to be heard by listening to others and seeking to understand their points of view

- Yielding expectations that certain requests or special days will be remembered

- Parents allowing the children to develop their gifts and interests instead of demanding that they meet unrealistic expectations

- Sons and daughters yielding their rights to choose their own friends, styles of clothing, music, and activities in order to fulfill their parents' wishes

I will...

- be slow to get angry.
- listen more than I talk.
- put others ahead of myself.
- stop arguments by yielding rights.
- control my reactions.

Rewards of Meekness

Understanding

More time listening instead of angrily speaking gives a person a greater understanding of others.

Strength

A person who yields his or her way in deference to another has much self-control. Being quick to hear another and slow to get angry requires much strength of character.

"Meekness takes injuries like pills, not chewing, but swallowing them down."

Sir Thomas Browne

OBEDIENCE

vs. Willfulness

Quickly and cheerfully carrying out the wise direction of those who are responsible for me

Obedience in the home includes:

- Establishing practical guidelines of good character for the family

- Parents teaching children why an activity is right or wrong

- Children understanding the purpose of guidelines and the consequences for failing to obey them

- Sons and daughters having the boldness to reject wrong actions in order to obey parents, despite other pressures

- Parents being role models to their children by honoring their own parents

Wood ducks are attentive to their parents' voices, even before they hatch. Twenty-four hours after hatching, they must obey their mother in jumping from their high nest, or they will be left behind to perish.

I will...

- obey my authorities immediately.
- have a cheerful attitude.
- complete all that I am expected to do.
- go the "extra mile."
- not obey a wrong command.

Rewards of Obedience

Protection
The road to success often includes painful lessons that obedience protects us from repeating.

Provision
Parents and other authorities enjoy rewarding an obedient spirit in those under them by giving to needs and wants.

Direction
An obedient spirit in sons and daughters motivates their parents to give the wisest possible counsel for the decisions they face.

"Obedience is much more seen in little things than in great."

Thomas Fuller

> "Good order is the foundation of all good things."
> Edmund Burke

vs. Confusion
ORDERLINESS

Arranging myself and my surroundings to achieve greater efficiency

Chipmunks spend their autumn days gathering seeds and nuts for the approaching winter. The food storage bins in a chipmunk's burrow are only one aspect of the carefully organized network of rooms and tunnels that make up its underground home.

Orderliness in the home includes:

- Planning a weekly schedule for personal and family activities

- Budgeting the income to meet each family member's needs

- Learning to take the time to put things back after using them

- Resisting the temptation to buy more than there is time, money, or space for

- Having a place for every possession and being willing to get rid of personal things in order to have sufficient space for everything

Rewards of Orderliness

Peace
Clutter produces tension, which robs a person of inner tranquility.

Achievement
Much time and energy are lost when necessary things cannot be found or are not in working condition.

Enjoyment
When clutter is removed, the possessions that remain are able to be enjoyed to their fullest.

─ I will... ─
- pick up after myself.
- keep my work and play areas clean and neat.
- put things back where they belong.
- use things only for their intended purposes.
- return lost things to their rightful owners.

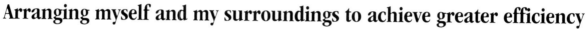

Patience in the home includes:

- Dealing with difficulties as character building opportunities instead of seeking to solve the family problems by making more money

- Being willing to make the most of a limited income

- Giving up immediate wants if they do not help the family as a whole

- Children being diligent to do their homework well even if the subject or teacher is difficult or unpleasant

Monarch butterflies migrate hundreds of miles to their wintering areas. There, the temperature needs to remain close to 32°F. This is warm enough so that the butterflies do not freeze but cold enough so that they remain inactive. The monarchs must wait and rest through the winter if they are to have enough strength for the long spring flight back home.

Patience vs. Restlessness

Accepting a difficult situation without giving a deadline to remove it

Rewards of Patience

Maturity

One measure of maturity is how long one can wait between achievement and reward.

Hope

Hope is the anticipation of good things to come. It is an important ingredient to a happy life. The enjoyment of a thing is increased when one has waited a long time to receive it.

"Haste makes waste."
Common saying

Heroes of Character

Hideyo Noguchi (1876–1928)

After falling into a fire at the age of three, Hideyo's hand was left completely useless. As he grew older, he realized that because of his handicap he could never be a successful farmer, the only occupation for a poor Japanese boy at that time.

He threw himself into his studies, working two jobs to pay for his schooling. Although he was mocked by his classmates because of his deformed hand, he still assisted them with their studies after he finished his own. When a skillful doctor performed a successful operation on his hand, Hideyo was so impressed that he decided to become a doctor.

The patience he developed as a result of his handicap, and the lessons he learned in his youth about working through difficulties, helped him to become an expert on the prevention of many diseases that ravaged the world, such as tetanus, trachoma, and bubonic plague. He died during an epidemic of yellow fever in Africa while working toward finding a cure for it.

Persuasiveness
vs. Contentiousness

Guiding vital truths around another's mental roadblocks

Persuasiveness in the home includes:

- A parent revealing how commitments to good character will strengthen the family and benefit each individual member
- Family members explaining how their cautions are not based on their own fears or selfish motives but on the family's best interest
- A parent showing children how wise decisions will protect them
- Older siblings motivating younger siblings by being good role models

The highly honored peacock is actually a kind of chicken. However, its beautiful plumage and stately bearing have won for it entry into the courts of royalty.

I will...

- point others in the right direction.
- not stretch the truth to make it more attractive.
- appeal to a person's conscience in terms of character.
- wait for the best time.
- not argue.

Rewards of Persuasiveness

Fellowship

When family members are able to persuade each other to do what is wise and right, they enjoy a fellowship that comes by being on the same side of a struggle.

Prosperity

The success of negotiation is based on one's ability to persuade all parties that they will mutually benefit.

Punctuality in the home includes:

- Giving priority to appointments made with family members

- Lifting the burdens of family members so they can get where they need to be, on time

- Being in the car in good time so as not to make the whole family late

- Family members going to bed on time in order to get up on time the next day

- Family members promptly responding to letters and phone calls

Punctuality
vs. Tardiness

Showing esteem for others by doing the right thing at the right time

Each year on March 19, migrating cliff swallows arrive in San Juan Capistrano, California, as they return north. Thousands of people gather in the small town to watch. Records honoring the punctuality of various species of swallows around the world exist from as long ago as 600 B.C.

"If time be of all things the most precious, wasting time must be the greatest prodigality."
Benjamin Franklin

Rewards of Punctuality

Respect
People count the faults of those who keep them waiting—the longer people wait, the more faults they can find.

Efficiency
Punctuality avoids the loss of time and energy that results from waiting and allows maximum teamwork for the task at hand.

I will...
- not wait until the last minute.
- be on time.
- allow extra time for delays.
- not keep others waiting.
- remember deadlines.

Muskies are not picky eaters. They will eat virtually anything smaller than themselves, including ducks, frogs, rats, squirrels, water snakes, and smaller fish. This large fish resourcefully feeds on that which others might consider useless or undesirable.

Resourcefulness in the home includes:

- Family members cherishing every moment together, however small, in order to build their relationships

- Wisely investing any extra income from overtime, holidays, and bonuses

- Finding creative ways to fix leftovers and foods the family has in abundance

- Using free time to enhance learning and creativity

- Finishing all the food on the plate before getting dessert

Rewards of Resourcefulness

Creativity

Requiring oneself to design new ways to use extra food, money, possessions, or time develops creativity.

Rich dividends

Making wise use of extra resources increases the value of those resources. Investing a small sum of money multiplies into a large sum over time; the same result is true of any resource wisely used.

I will...

- reuse what I can.
- not waste food.
- repair what is broken.
- recycle.
- give away or sell what I do not use.

Resourcefulness
vs. Wastefulness

Finding practical uses for that which others would overlook or discard

"Everything in the world is good for something."
Dryden

Responsibility in the home includes:

- Parents diligently working to provide for the family

- Accepting the challenge of making the household run as smoothly and efficiently as possible

- A parent giving a child encouragement and advice

- Children obeying and honoring their parents in actions, words, and body language

- Developing skills to the best of one's ability

Responsibility
vs. Unreliability

Knowing and doing what is expected of me

From its lofty perch, the magnificent bald eagle is able to keep a sharp lookout over its entire domain. With its keen eyesight, the eagle can investigate unusual disturbances a mile below as it soars through the sky.

Rewards of Responsibility

Trust

When a person completes the work he or she is given to do, this person will gain trust from others. His or her good reputation will open the door for increased responsibility.

Profit

People will reap what they sow; if they are negligent in their work, they will reap nothing in reward. However, people who do what is expected of them will reap a profit greater than the effort they put into their work.

I will...

- keep my promises.
- do my best.
- be accountable for my actions.
- do my duty with honor.
- not make excuses.

> "People want something against which they can lean back and know that it will never give."
> Robert J. McCracken

Trust in God

Security *vs. Anxiety*

Structuring my life around that which cannot be destroyed or taken away

The safest place for a newborn kangaroo is in its mother's pouch. There it finds all the warmth, protection, and food it needs without fear. Even after they grow old enough to venture outside, young "joeys,"as they are called, always have a secure place of retreat.

Security in the home includes:

- A parent conquering fear of aging by investing his or her life into serving the children, creating a legacy that will outlast him or her

- Developing friendships with each other by playing games, laughing, and talking together

- Sons and daughters developing their character and life skills instead of worrying over future training and work

- Family members focusing on building relationships rather than collecting material possessions

I will...

- invest my time in things that last.
- build my skills and character.
- not depend on money for happiness.
- correct unsafe conditions.
- not worry about other people's concerns.

Rewards of Security

Contentment
Investing time and energy into developing relationships and building character frees a person from the fear of losing possessions, fame, health, or youthfulness.

Vision
Focusing on what cannot be taken away or destroyed gives greater insight into life and gives a vision for the future.

Self-Control

vs. Self-Indulgence

Rejecting wrong desires and doing what is right

Self-control in the home includes:

- Family members controlling their tempers and resolving any anger they might have

- Being careful to speak words that would only encourage and not tear down one another, even when irritated

- Parents instilling in their children the good habits of proper nutrition, vigorous exercise, rising early, and following a structured daily schedule

Unlike the hibernating woodchuck or ground squirrel, the black bear can arouse from its four-month slumber if danger threatens its cubs.

I will...

- think before I act.
- take care of my body.
- sit still in class.
- control my temper.
- not give in to do wrong.

Rewards of Self-control

Freedom

Daily practicing positive habits and disciplines gives a person freedom from bad habits.

Fortitude

Picture a fortress with walls that are broken down. The army inside no longer has strength or fortitude to fight the enemy. In this same way, when people allow their anger to burst out uncontrollably, they weaken themselves. Those who learn to control their temper build strength and fortitude.

"If thou wilt conquer thy weakness thou must not gratify it."
William Penn

"The best portions of a good man's life are his little, nameless, unremembered acts of kindness and love."

Unknown

I will...

- listen to others fully.
- watch facial expressions.
- notice tone of voice.
- put myself in others' shoes.
- show that I care.

Sensitivity in the home includes:

- Realizing that a family member's irritating behavior may be a sign of an unmet need for love
- Noticing when a family member needs a word of praise instead of another problem to fix
- A parent being alert to attitudes of hurt, guilt, and disloyalty in the children
- Parents realizing that the seeds of a wounded spirit in a child can grow up into a crop of rebellion
- Being aware that rude words deeply hurt one another

Sensitivity
vs. Callousness

Perceiving the true attitudes and emotions of those around me

Rewards of Sensitivity

Perception
The more a person is sensitive to the needs of others, the more perception he will gain in all areas of life.

Purpose
Those who refresh others will themselves be refreshed. Refreshment comes from being sensitive to others which gives life fresh meaning and purpose.

The highly sensitive ears of the snowshoe rabbit can hear faint noises and accurately determine the source of the sound. The rabbit's nose is also very keen, helping it to locate food.

> **"What you seem to be, be really."**
> Benjamin Franklin

Sincerity
vs. Hypocrisy

Eagerness to do what is right, with transparent motives

I will...

- be all that I can be.
- take responsibility for my own actions.
- respect others' opinions.
- always mean what I say.
- not take advantage of other people.

A beehive is an intricate colony with thousands of bees living in a delicate balance of cooperation. Clear and sincere communication between the bees in a hive is vital for the effectiveness and survival of them all.

Sincerity in the home includes:

- Treating family members the same at home as in public
- Family members upholding in the home the same standards they represent to others
- Sons and daughters doing things of which their parents would approve, even when with friends
- Family members discussing people as if those people were present

Rewards of Sincerity

Honor
To the same degree that people despise hypocrites, they honor those who are sincere and have integrity.

Trust
When people see that our motives are transparent and that we have a sincere desire to do what is right, they will put great trust in what we think and say.

Thoroughness
vs. Incompleteness

The American alligator makes careful preparations for its young, not overlooking any details. The female clears a choice site for her nest, builds it to precise specifications, and maintains its integrity until her young safely hatch.

I will...

- plan my work.
- pay attention to details.
- make a list so I don't forget.
- finish what I start.
- clean up before I quit.

Knowing what factors will diminish the effectiveness of my work or words, if neglected

Thoroughness in the home includes:

- Avoiding leaving appliances partially fixed or tools broken
- Parents requiring the children to clean under furniture and behind shelves
- Sons and daughters calling home when they are out too late
- Children completing homework using legible handwriting
- Family members having a system of receiving phone messages and passing them on accurately

Rewards of Thoroughness

Fulfillment
A special sense of fulfillment is experienced when a job has been done completely.

Creativity
The need to be thorough within time limits stimulates creativity and inventiveness.

"He who despiseth little things shall perish by little and little."

Proverb

Heroes of Character

George Washington Carver (1861–1943)

As a young boy, George Washington Carver learned the importance of not neglecting work and study to enjoy his love of nature and painting. This thoroughness in keeping his priorities straight later paid off when he became a botanist and chemist.

As the professor of agriculture at the Tuskegee Institute, he was approached by farmers asking him to help them restore their depleted fields to productivity. After careful research, he found that peanuts would be the best crop to plant. However, when the peanuts were harvested, the farmers found that there was no market for their abundant crop. Feeling responsible, Professor Carver determined to create a market and go all the way in helping the farmers. After only two days, he found twenty new uses for the peanut. Not satisfied with this, he continued researching throughout his lifetime, discovering over three hundred uses for the peanut, including peanut butter!

Thriftiness *vs. Extravagance*

Allowing myself and others to spend ONLY what is necessary

Because a koala's diet of eucalyptus leaves provides so little nutrition, the small mammal spends its precious energy very carefully. To avoid exhaustion, it moves slowly between branches to save as much strength as possible.

Thriftiness in the home includes:

- Budgeting the income and formulating family guidelines by which to evaluate each expenditure

- Avoiding the temptation of sales and excessive shopping in order to stick to a budget

- A parent showing the children how to budget money and schedule priorities and goals

- Investing personal money and time wisely in order to prepare for future goals

Rewards of Thriftiness

Provision
By avoiding unnecessary expenditures, a family will have enough money to make essential major purchases that everyone can enjoy.

Achievement
Prioritizing one's activities will enable a person to avoid spending time and energy on projects that are not important. As a result, one will accomplish the big things, and the little things will usually take care of themselves.

> "Thrift is good revenue."
> H. G. Bohn

I will...

- save more and spend less.
- make good use of what I already have.
- look for the best value.
- budget my money, time, and energy.
- not confuse what I need with what I want.

64

Tolerance in the home includes:

- Focusing on family members' strengths instead of their weaknesses
- A parent realizing that each child will grow and develop good character at different levels of enthusiasm and maturity
- Parents not showing favoritism to certain children
- Sons and daughters accepting that parents are still growing in character and are not perfect
- Family members being patient with each other

"With all thy faults, I love thee still."
— William Cowper

Rewards of Tolerance

Discernment

Realizing that other people have different convictions and levels of maturity enables a person to have greater discernment of another's true needs.

Acceptance

Discerning another's needs rather than judging his or her character flaws shows the other person care and acceptance. A person who accepts others will receive the same acceptance in spite of personal flaws.

The soft meat of the eastern box turtle is a delicacy for curious raccoons. Unable to fight against the agile raccoon, the turtle must retreat inside its shell. As the raccoon tinkers with the turtle, trying to find a crack to pry it open, the turtle must patiently tolerate being turned over and tossed around while holding itself shut.

Tolerance
vs. Prejudice

Realizing that everyone is at varying levels of character development

I will...

- look beyond appearances.
- accept people for who they are.
- help others grow in character.
- look at myself first.
- not confuse what is right with what is popular.

TRUTHFULNESS *vs. Deception*

Earning future trust by accurately reporting past facts

The African lion is feared by other animals and by people. Its power and majesty are revered by all. On the plains of Africa, young boys became men only by an act of bravery. Many times this required them to slay an African lion. The boys learned how to respond to a lion's body language. They knew a lion's intentions by the way the big cat hung its head or displayed its teeth.

Truthfulness in the home includes:

- Being transparent with one another, knowing that respect is won, not by hiding, but by confessing, faults

- Revealing the exact amount of money spent on purchases instead of only how much was saved

- Sons and daughters giving their parents all the details about questionable activities so parents will have the correct impression of the people and conditions involved

- Not exaggerating facts to impress one another

Rewards of Truthfulness

Clear conscience

Deception results in guilt, with its physical, emotional, mental, and spiritual consequences. Truthfulness produces boldness and confidence.

Trust

Truthfulness is the foundation of integrity and evokes trust from others.

VIRTUE *vs. Impurity*

The moral excellence evident in my life as I consistently do what is right

Before the enactment of protective legislation, the great white egret was nearly pushed to extinction. Their pure white plumes actually reached a point of greater value per ounce than gold.

Virtue in the home includes:

- A parent establishing a standard of moral conduct in the family and upholding it by example
- A parent teaching children to make wise choices about friends, music, and clothing
- Family members dressing modestly, inside and outside the home
- Family members filling their minds with uplifting music and good influences

Rewards of Virtue

Family blessing

Parents who keep their eyes from evil and their minds from impure thoughts will not only receive blessing in their own lives but also in the lives of their children. Their own past failures are less likely to be repeated in their children's lives.

Opportunities

The counsel of those who have overcome past failures is sought by others who are dealing with similar problems.

I will...

- do what is right and encourage others to do the same.
- guard my eyes, ears, words, and thoughts.
- learn to stand alone.
- abstain from anything which might damage or pollute my mind or body.
- treat others as I would want them to treat me.

"Riches adorn the dwelling; virtue adorns the person."

Chinese proverb

Wisdom vs. Foolishness

Making practical applications of truth in daily decisions

Wisdom in the home includes:

- Seeking each other's counsel and avoiding rash decisions
- Seeing the family structure as an essential element of family harmony
- Protecting the family by visualizing the consequences of foolish decisions and determining how to avoid them
- Seeking a wise and understanding group of friends
- Sons and daughters choosing friends of whom their parents approve
- Family members learning from the examples of wise people

For centuries, the great horned owl has been regarded as a symbol of wisdom. One reason is because the owl has two large, round eyes; sharp hearing; and one very small mouth.

I will...

- listen to my parents and teachers.
- learn from correction.
- choose my friends carefully.
- remember there are consequences to all my actions.
- ask, "What is the right thing to do?"

Rewards of Wisdom

Discretion

Looking at present situations with a wise perspective gives insight and discretion for making future decisions that will bring desirable consequences and rewards.

Success

A wise person will see the benefits and dangers of various courses of action and will choose the one that will result in success. The problems and pitfalls that hinder the simpleminded will be avoided.

Achieving True Success

"There is an indissoluble union between virtue and happiness."
George Washington

Rewards of Building Character . . .

How to Build Character as a Family

How do Character Families fit into a bigger picture?

"No nation can be destroyed while it possesses a good home life."—Josiah Gilbert Holland

HAVE YOU EVER FELT FRUSTRATED because you were truly trying to instill in your children positive qualities, but felt that you were fighting against the tide of our current culture? That everything you were trying to build was being torn down as soon as your son or daughter walked out the front door?

We have good news for you: it does not have to be that way. City and state leaders around the world are catching the vision for creating a community culture where good character is encouraged and rewarded. They have pioneered a plan to integrate character training programs into every sector of the community, including city government, schools, businesses, the faith community, and the media. As the community focuses on one character quality per month, people get excited about how they can be involved, new ideas are generated, and the effort multiplies.

Imagine your children coming home from school . . . singing a song about how truthfulness is "gaining future trust by accurately reporting past facts." Imagine your son going up to clean his room . . . so he can be like an orderly chipmunk. Imagine your daughter settling a dispute on the playground . . . because she had studied forgiveness that month. Imagine going to work and being praised by your supervisor . . . not so much for making that big sale, but for demonstrating initiative and creativity on the job. Imagine your young adult son coming home from work all aglow . . . because his boss took a personal interest in his employees and shared with them the rewards of attentiveness.

These are only a few of the stories from cities whose leaders have officially resolved to make their cities known as Cities of Character. The International Association of Character Cities (IACC) was formed in April 1998 as a service organization to support leaders who desire to promote a community consensus of universally recognized character qualities. The IACC facilitates communication among city leaders and provides resources, training, and assistance for community character initiatives. Through the IACC, leaders are able to share information, ideas, and solutions for strengthening their own character and the character of those they serve. Together we are . . .

Building Cities of Character™

. . . family by family.

An effective CHARACTER CITY in a nutshell

law enforcement

city government

the workplace

schools

faith community

media

▪ Character Family
The family is the hub around
which the Character City revolves.

▪ character in city government
Government officials and employees lead the way by
example for character training in the community.

▪ character in the workplace
Fathers and mothers receive character training in
their places of work and bring resources home for
use in their own families.

▪ character in schools
Children learn the same character qualities at
school, so that home and school training
complement each other.

▪ character in the faith community
Qualities that parents are instilling in their
children are being reinforced and deepened at
the family's place of worship.

▪ character highlighted by the media
The media creates an atmosphere throughout the
community that encourages and rewards good
character.

▪ character in law enforcement
Police officers model the character they enforce
and focus on building relationships with members
of the community.

What is a CHARACTER CITY?

Mayors and city councils across America
and throughout the world are voting to
become Character Cities. Leaders rep-
resenting each sector of the community
then form a committee to design ways of
promoting one character quality each
month— qualities such as initiative,
diligence, punctuality, gratefulness,
truthfulness, and generosity. The result
is a community consensus to live by
time-honored and universally recognized character qualities.

*. . . It is at the family
level, however, that any
lasting, positive, societal
change will occur.*

For more information about building **Cities of Character**, visit
www.charactercities.org or e-mail info@charactercities.org.

**"We seek to
prevent crime
by inspiring
virtue at an
early age."**
Daniel Webster

71

Building Character . . .
From the Ground Up

"We build character!"

The Larios Children—plus two!
First Official Character Family

ur family has for many years had the desire to benefit our community, serve government leaders, encourage other families, and build family unity and character, but we had never seen how these pieces fit together. We were excited about the Character Cities and Character States concept and were thinking about what we could do to promote character in our community.

We decided that if a Character State was made up of Character Cities, wouldn't a Character City be made up of "Character Families"? This seemed to finally fit all of the pieces together: centering everything we wanted to do around the concept of being a "Family of Character."

Character development has always been important to my parents. Our chores are referred to as "character builders," and they have always been careful to make sure that we are surrounded by good influences and have friends who encourage us to build good character, rather than develop negative attitudes and habits. While they have always been alert to "character deficiencies," they are also quick to praise us when we demonstrate good character.

However, it was not until my sister Sara returned in May from working with the International Association of Character Cities that we finally put our "Character Family" idea into action.

Laying a Solid Foundation

Sara and I both have worked as legislative aides at the state capitol, so our family is very familiar with the legislative process. We decided to make our "Family of Character" official by writing a resolution. When our "family council" met to discuss the resolution, Dad told us, "We are not just going to sign this and stick it on the refrigerator and forget about it. By adopting this resolution, we are committing to implement everything in it."

We passed and signed the resolution, which gave us a permanent reminder of our decision. A "Character

Committee," made up of all the family members over the age of twelve, was formed and began meeting weekly, writing a mission statement to guide us, and forming a strategy.

Getting Down to Nuts 'n' Bolts

Our next step was to make sure that we kept character in the

by Rachel Larios

forefront to *communicate* good character. We designed character awareness projects to reinforce character training and keep character qualities and their definitions in plain view.

GENEROSITY

"When I draw the posters about the character qualities it makes me feel good, because they remind my brothers and sisters to not be naughty," said eight-year-old Micah.

We set up a "media team." Micah, aged eight, is in charge of posting decorated character posters in prominent places, such as the refrigerator, bathroom mirrors, etc. I send out "press releases" to update family and friends on our community service projects.

Our parents were certain to emphasize that the older siblings should lead the way and that the good example of an older brother or sister is powerful in younger siblings' lives. While Dad and Mom can model good character in a parent, only brothers and sisters can be models of boys, girls, and young people with exemplary character.

One Story Upon Another

As our excitement built, we started sharing with other families about what we were doing and looked for ways to spread this enthusiasm into the community.

One of our first projects as a Character Family was to approach our county library director about

We helped teach Character First!® at the county library one day a week for their summer reading program.

teaching Character First!® as part of the summer reading program. Little did we know what an overwhelming response we would receive from members of the community who attended and from the library staff. Teaching this program has opened many doors of opportunity, and each opportunity, when acted upon, leads to another.

One of my brothers' favorite character-building activities is to go with my dad and pick up trash from the sides of the road. Sometimes people stop and thank them, and many people who meet us later or already know our family have expressed their gratefulness. Some think they are a Boy Scout troop!

A New Vantage Point

Being a Character Family has also helped me see that people really

My brother Gideon, aged six, said, "My favorite character quality to work on is orderliness, because it helps me not to have a messy room."

appreciate things that might seem small to us—such as turning in coins that we find on the floor in the store. My brothers have gotten wonderful responses when they have turned in money. The people are surprised but encouraged, and we are encouraged too. Also, complimenting people on their diligence, attentiveness, kindness, and so on makes them so appreciative.

Becoming a Character Family has brought our family together as we strive to build character in our own lives and in the lives of those around us.

"We are overwhelmed by what has come from this idea, but we are also excited because this is something that we can use to encourage other families," my dad said. "It's going to

be a challenge—we've set our goals high—but if we're all committed, I believe we can reach those goals. This has been a turning point for our family—it makes me as a father more accountable. It makes a difference in everything: how we treat each other, our behavior, our entire lives."

Or as Jesse, aged three, put it, "I'm a Character Boy!"

Character under construction

Bob and Carolyn Larios have seven children, Sara (20), Rachel (16), Luke (13), Jacob (10), Micah (8), Gideon (6), and Jesse (3). For the past two summers, they have hosted two Russian orphans, Sergei (12) and Fyoder (8).

Rewards of Being a Character Family

for the Larios family

"This program has been a turning point for our family—it makes me as a father more accountable. It makes a difference in everything: how we treat each other, our behavior, our entire lives."

Mr. Bob Larios

"It makes us want to do more and more jobs!"

Gideon, age 6

Being a Character Family...

- **builds family unity,** because it is a program that involves the entire family. It develops a lifelong priority on character, because character is something that everyone can continue to improve and work on at any age.

- **increases opportunities.** Character is the number one thing that employers, government leaders, and others are looking for in prospective employees. Employers can teach people new skills, but there is no substitute for a person of outstanding character.

The number one comment our family has received when the children have gone to work at the capitol or other settings has not been about their skills but about their character.

- **brings joy** as joy is brought to others. The results encourage everyone.

  C.g. When we go out at Christmastime and give meals and baked goods to those in need, we also sing Christmas carols to them. Many cry and say that no one has ever sung to them before.

- **gives us a new perspective on work.** The drudgery of chores is exchanged for the challenge of "character builders." This perspective also helps us look at our home as a place to keep in constant readiness for the purpose of hospitality.

- **increases accountability.** If others know you are a Character Family, children are more aware that others are observing them and learning from their example. This provides extra motivation for them to obey.

  C.g. We often hear the comment from one of the children to another, "If you act naughty, no one else will want to be in a Character Family!"

- **turns the hearts of children** to their parents as their "character coaches" as they introduce character qualities and projects.

- **encourages us to do good in the community** and be proactive instead of waiting for others to do something. We had no idea this would open up so many opportunities.

- **builds a better community and nation.** The character developed in the home forms the character of the nation. Parents shape the character of society by shaping the character of their own children. The character each home builds or fails to build affects every area of our society.

Any Family
Can Build Character

"Growing up in a poor area in the suburbs of Los Angeles without a father, I (Bob) did not feel myself adequately prepared to take on the role of father. I knew that I wanted to raise my children to be men and women of high moral character, but I did not feel that I personally met that description or that I was equipped to do so. However, I was at least willing to try and committed to doing whatever it took.

"My wife Carolyn also grew up in the inner city of L.A. Throughout our marriage, we have faced many crises, from being unemployed and having to live in an old farmhouse without heat, to losing our first son at the age of one. We have weathered very serious illnesses in ourselves and our children, plus a cross-country move, but we can look back and see how character was being developed in all of us. We have tried to base our decisions and responses on character rather than feelings or emotions.

"Character training works! My children now have character that I never had at their ages. If anything, our family is a living example that *anyone* can build a Family of Character."

74

A Resolution

"Character is the ability to carry out a good resolution
long after the excitement of the moment has passed."
Robert Cavett

Whereas we recognize our own
needs and inadequacies and desire to develop
wholesome relationships with each member of our family
and be of benefit to our community,

we hereby declare

the _____ family

to be a

Character Family

with the goals of

Learning how to apply specific character qualities,

Developing daily habits to establish good character,

Turning needs and conflicts into "character classrooms," and

Demonstrating character by serving others.

Signed this _____ day of _____, _____

Family members:

Building Families *of* Character™

IACC™
INTERNATIONAL ASSOCIATION
OF CHARACTER CITIES